04/24/2010

Horse Behaviour
Book 1 The Nature of Horses

Sid Gustafson
Doctor of Veterinary Medicine
Equine Behaviour Educator

Table of Contents

Foreword 4

The Merging of Horses and Humans 7

Welcome to a Horse's World 10

Born to Graze 12

Born to Travel 14

Born to Know 17

Born to Socialize 21

Born to Communicate 23

Born to Please 35

Born to Friend 33

Born to Play 38

Born to Mingle 42

Born to Move 46

Born to Graze 56

Born to Heal 52

Born to Run 58

Equine Behaviour and the Practice of Veterinary Medicine 63

References 81

In Conclusion 83

Dedicated to all the horses I have known.
Thank you Jake.

Figure 1 Dr Sid atop his favorite horse Jake, deep in the Montana wilderness.

Foreword

This writing is a science-based primer on the nature of horses. *Horse Behaviour* is a guide to help horsefolk keep their horses happy and healthy. It is a treatise for those seeking to develop willing partnerships with their equine companions.

Understanding the nature of horses is the first step to successful horsemanship. To teach horses, we must know them.

Through time horses have embedded themselves into the psyche of humans in a variety of cultures throughout the world. Linguists proclaim that the ancient words for mind and horse are similar in a variety of horse societies. The Mongol word for horse is *takh*, meaning spirit. The original horse people related to horses in a state of flowing communication. The result was a blending of human society with horse society. After eons of walking across the world, humans brought the wild Tarpan into their fold. As the two species came closer and closer together, the original horsepeople tamed, trained, and selectively bred the Tarpan to become today's horse.

The process of domestication required eons of time; a blending of species brought about a shared geography and shared communication. Each species observed and followed the other for millennia, developing an understanding that resulted in a sophisticated merger. The domestication process continues to this day. To blend with horses, people must know horses. Here we will come to appreciate the deepest natures of the horse, the natures that allowed this wonderful species to blend with us.

Sustenance of this blending of horse and human requires an appreciation of the nature of the horses. The once daily and hourly coexistence has drifted. A rift has developed. If a contemporary horseperson seeks unity with horses, they must come to know the horse in order to bridge the rift.

Figure 2 The Centaur exemplifies mankind's long held desire to blend with the horse, to become the horse.

Today, horsefolk attempt to develop willing partnerships with horses as the original domesticators must have. Appreciation of equine behaviour allows this blending, which can be quite real.

In order to develop a reliable horse, lessons have to be taught and retaught, and taught again. Repetition is key. Not only do horses learn like humans, humans learn like horses. In light of that, my writing will often involve a repetition of certain concepts. I teach equine behavior by repetition, much as I teach horses. Concepts, sentences, ideas, and chapters will be repeated time and again. Repetition is how horses learn, and it is a method I have found succeeds with humans, as well.

The Merging of Horses and Humans

Convergent social and communicative characteristics drew humans and horses together. In a sophisticated blending of group survival, horse merged into humankind's social structure ten thousand years ago or so. Our contemporary relationship with horses as companions and performers can be aptly appreciated through an understanding of the evolutionary processes that impelled horses and humans to come together in the first place. Shared social traits and communication abilities continue to facilitate a mutually beneficial existence. Horses are like humans. These days, horses continue to sustain mankind's dreams. Horses allow us to maintain our connection with nature. To know the social sphere of horses allows people to enter that sphere. Horsemanship remains slipping into the horse's social circle, to pair bond with the animal.

The domestication process began tens of thousands of years ago when groups of horses and Neolithic people began sharing the grasslands of northern Eurasia. Before merging their groups together, horses and humans and dogs independently developed the communication and social skills to enhance group survival via family living. Similar social goals facilitated a merging of mankind with dog and horse. Group survival became shared group survival. Dogs provided protection. Dogs and people cleared the grasslands of predators. Interested horses came closer, and became more tolerant, reaping the grazing safety the dogs procured.

The pursuit of horses shifted to the herding of horses, which led to their taming, milking, breeding and riding. Unlike some domestic species, each and every horse requires training to become useful. In knowing horses, we can train them easily.

To grasp how man and horse societies likely merged long ago is to appreciate the contemporary horse/rider relationship. To develop positive relationships with the horse, one must come into an awareness of the long evolved social skills of horses. Horsemanship merges human nature with the nature of the horse. The language of horsemanship allows horses and humans to achieve pairings that exceed the sum of horse and rider.

The social nature of horses is one of constant awareness. Humans are required to come into an awareness of horses, to know their behaviour. Constant awareness is essential for group survival. The landscape must be surveyed as the group grazes collectively connected. Cooperative partnerships facilitate the blending of horse and rider many seek. Horses living in harems in natural settings remain constantly aware of all the other horses in the herd; behaviours are learned and taught within this society of horses. Humans must slip into the horse's social construct to succeed with horses. Horses are born to learn. Awareness is essential for learning. Here we will become aware of the horse and all her nuances.

Welcome to the Horse's World

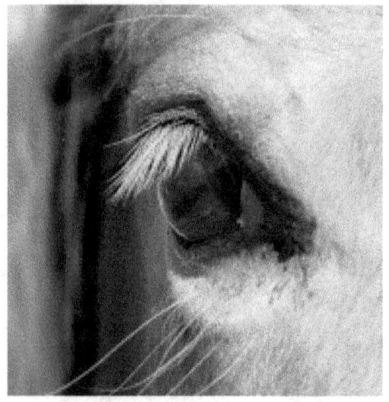

Figure 3   Sophisticated Horsemanship requires learning to see as the horse sees

Most horses are innately fearful of all new things. This is normal and expected behaviour. Horses constantly survey their surroundings with their stellar vision. They listen and smell. They see by day or night, with a field of vision approaching 360°. Eyes set high in their head, horses graze and gaze, they watch and eat, and this is their deepest nature. The grazing nipping and chewing motion rotates their head enough to see behind them with each bite. When not grazing or dozing, horses focus on watching. When dozing or sleeping, others horses watch for them.

All horses need other horses to sustain behavioural health. Foals raised by the mare and herd in a grazing setting develop into easily trainable animals. The herd socialization process teaches growing horses how to be horses, and it is horses that humans are inherently born to teach and train.

The mare and herd give growing horses the confidence to interact with others, be they horse or human. Horses learn how to learn from other horses. The herd teaches young horses to learn, to move, to see and graze, and perhaps most importantly, to communicate with others. This is socialization. Socialization is essential for behavioural health, and it is the social circle of horses that horsetrainers must slip into to develop willing partnerships.

Horses keep an eye on people, a very keen and knowing eye. Here, we are going to learn how to keep an eye on horses. Together, we shall come to see the world as horses see our world. With that wisdom we can enhance our ability to develop willing partnerships with horses. By appreciating the horse's long-evolved nature as social grazers of the plains, we can more readily and consistently keep horses happy, healthy, and willing to learn. In a sense, we will learn how to become part of their herd, an integral addition to their society of group survivalists.

Born to Graze

Doing Right by Horses

The notion of equine welfare features prominently in this book. Equine behaviour is the basis of equine welfare. By coming to know horses, we learn to care for horses in a considerate fashion in light of their long-evolved preferences and needs. Everything that horses are, and everything horses become is under the control of humans. Humankind is compelled to care for horses in a humane fashion. Horses are a result of the care than man affords horses. There are no malevolent horses, as horses are a creation of the breeding and care they are afforded by mankind. Each and every horse is the horse humans have made him or her.

Horse breeders and caretakers need to care for horses in appropriate fashion, to do right by them. Horses are responsible for the development of civilization as we know it. Horses did not create civilization, but they provided the transportation and drayage to deliver civilization into the eventual sophisticated state that we now enjoy.

Mankind is obligated to take care of horses in an appropriate fashion. Humans are morally directed to provide appropriate care for horses. Five areas of the horse's nature need addressed each and every day. As the guardians and caretakers of horses, we are impelled to provide horses with

1) An appropriate environment.

2) The appropriate sociobehavioural circumstances.

3) Appropriate nutrition.

4) Appropriate teaching and training.

5) Appropriate selective breeding.

6) Appropriate veterinary care.

Figure 4 Curiosity toward Humankind, a primary domestication 'sugar.' Horses like horsey people. Domestication 'sugars' are the traits that horses share with humans, and there are many. Rather than different than humans, horses are much like humans. In many ways, horses and humans learn, teach, share, and live alike.

Born to Travel

Journeys with Horses

Figure 5 Waiting under the glacier to ride across the bottom of sea. Iceland

As you read this book you will begin your equine behaviour journey unknowing what awaits you, much as horses began their journey through time 60 million years ago as they emerged after the dinosaur extinction. Three million years ago the footsteps of man were fossilized next to the hoofprints of horses in what is now

Kenya, suggesting that humans have been contemplating horses for some time. But it was not until perhaps ten to twenty thousand years ago that man began the dance of domestication with horse, the horse that became *Equus caballus.*

There is archeological evidence that man formed an intimate relationship with horses 5500 years ago in Botai, Kazakhstan. In this realm, horsefolk initially stabled and milked horses, and soon rode them. This domestic relationship began after millennia of human pursuit. Although the archeological evidence confirms 5500 years of domestication, the relationship began thousands of years earlier.

Both trained and wild horses came to exist in this open domain south of Russia and west of China, thus the horse retains much of her wild nature. Trained horses spread throughout the world, civilization of humankind being one notable result. By the early 20th century the predecessor to man's newest animal partner, the Tarpan, had gone extinct. No truly wild caballine horses remain. To the best of our knowledge, all horses today are descended from tamed and selectively bred horses. One gauge of domestication is the extinction of the progenitor, and mankind has managed that with horses and cattle. The horse of today is with us to stay. She can live with humans, or without them, and her wild nature remains. To succeed with horses is to know them, and all their wildness.

Horsefolk remain intrigued by horses. We find ourselves attempting to appreciate how the human/horse merger came to be.

We seek to sustain the continuum, much as mankind has sought since the first girl grabbed a mane and swung on a horse to become a partner with the flighty grazer of the plains.

My students tell me that Equine Behaviour differs from the other subjects in that I teach this discipline from the horse's perspective, while others teach equine science from the human perspective. This is true. In this guide, I represent the health and welfare of horses. I teach how to make training and stabling a good deal for the horse.

Equine behaviourists understand that appreciation and sensitivity to all of our horses' evolved preferences result in optimum health and soundness. Optimum health and happiness translate into optimum training and performance.

Horses need to grow up to be horses as taught by horses to eventually lead behaviourally healthy lives with humans. When grown, horses should be allowed to be horses with other horses. When stabled, natural must be re-created for the horse. The last place a horse evolved to live is in a stall. When horses are stalled, we are obligated to re-create their constant requirements of friends, forage, and locomotion.

Born to Know

A Quiet Moving Species
Born to Learn

Horses are a quiet species. They prefer calm, and learn most efficiently in tranquil, familiar settings. While horses readily adapt to noisy places, their preference is quiet. What may be music to humans is often noise to horses. Horses need to hear to be content, as hearing is a long-evolved survival characteristic, as are vision, taste, smell, and feel. All of these sensation abilities need expression.

We all know what we want from our horses, however in this primer of equine behaviour we will study the science of what our horses want and need from us, the science of equine behaviour. To succeed in our endeavors with horses (whatever equine goals or pursuits), our horses are best served to receive what they preferentially need and want behaviourally, nutritionally, socially, physically, environmentally, sensually, and metabolically. In order to properly care for horses and successfully teach horses, we must know them, the diligent social grazers of the plains they are.

Rather than dissimilar to us, horses are much like us. The

'horses are prey-humans are predators' concept is an ill-founded concept. In this book we will focus on humankind's social and communicative similarities to horses. Here, we embrace humankind's similarities to horses. As with people, a strong interdependence develops between individual horses resulting in intense social pair and herd bonds. Horses need other horses the same as humans need other humans. I term the traits shared by horses and humans 'sugars.' Domestication sugars are simply the similarities horses share with humans. Sugars facilitated the merger of horses and humans. All domesticate species are social species. Domestication requires a certain shared sociality. Sugars are metaphors for alikeness. Communication and social skills are sugars. Learning and teaching are domestication sugars.

Horses are born to move, in moving they know their world.

A deep and significant interdependence exists between health and locomotion. Horses evolved to be near-constant walkers and grazers. Horse health remains dependent on locomotion and grazing, or facsimiles thereof. If horses are not allowed to exercise freely, or socialize with other familiar horses nibbling and chewing as they evolved to do, they develop strategies to maintain the motion and oral security they need to survive. When horses are deprived of adequate friends, forage, and locomotion, they develop stereotypies to replace these survival requirements. Here, we do not call behaviours such as cribbing vices, as vices infer the horse is at fault. In this treatise, we will learn who is really at fault, and it is not the horse but rather the humans in charge of their development and husbandry. When behaviourists observe cribbing horses, they know that the humans deprived the horse of necessary forage one time too often. Horses require forage to chew on a near-constant basis to maintain behavioral and digestive health.

A primary premise of equine behavioural health is this: In natural settings, horses walk and graze together most all of the time. They take a step and graze several nips of forage, take another step or two, always moving, always observing their surroundings, keeping in touch with other members of the herd. In natural scenarios, horses never fast longer than three hours, and most never fast longer than one hour. A horse chews 70-90 times a minute for 16 to 20 hours a day. When any horse's essential forage, friends, and locomotion are restricted or deprived to a degree that exceeds their adaptability, physical and behavioural problems of all sorts begin to surface.

Figure 6 Born to Graze

Horses that are not afforded the opportunity to graze and walk and commune with others much of the time develop default behaviours to replicate these essential natures. When stabled in an inappropriate fashion, some of the horse's long-evolved survival behaviours become unwanted and unwelcome. Horses need to chew and move to live. It is essential that these natures are fulfilled in abundance if horsefolk want to keep their horses happy and healthy.

Away we graze, moving through our coursework as a herd of horses might graze open range, connectedly, in communication with one another, learning, forever learning.

Born to Socialize

Shared Social Structures

Horses and Humans are Quite Alike

Through a sophisticated refinement of group survival, horse and dog became domesticates, merging with mankind and enhancing their chances for survival. Man did not domesticate horse and dog by capturing them outright. Dog and horse came to mankind as much as humans came to them. Certain clades of horses and wolves chose to follow humans, eventually entering the same social realm.

Group survival is the primary nature of the horse. Unfortunately, it seems that too many people have been taught the unbalanced theory of survival of the fittest *individual*. Individual survival is not a theory that fits with the social structure of free ranging horses or wolves. Horses and wolves and humans are group survivalists by nature. They cooperate with one another to augment the survival of all. Appreciating how group survival brought horses and humans together is the key to appreciating the contemporary concepts of equine horsemanship.

Horse society is replete with organization. Everyone has a role, and the entire herd maintains a dynamic constant connection to facilitate survival of the herd in deference to the survival of the individual. Humans who come to fathom the depth of this conceit are the humans who blend effectively with horses. The nature of horses is to form strong pair bonds. True unity between horse and human is an interspecies pair bonding. It takes two to bond.

In natural settings, group-survival is the preference and the norm. The fittest species, group, herd, or harem survives.

In examining equine behaviour, the information we want to know and appreciate is how horses interact and communicate socially in those natural settings where horses are most at ease. We can apply this information to the training and teaching of horses. In the stable, where resources are limited, horses behave in a different, unnatural fashion. Stable behaviour is abnormal behaviour. The horse behaviour that is observed in confinement is not the sort of behaviour that can be applied to training, as this behaviour is a result of deprivation.

In natural settings, horses practice group survival. Space and forage are unlimited. There is no need to compete for resources. In natural settings we observe a cooperative existence. It is this cooperative existence that allows humans to slip in and teach and train horses. Horsemanship involves cooperation between the horse and human, as cooperation is the nature of the horse.

People who win with horses utilize behavioural knowledge of the nature of the horse to prevail in competitive pursuits. When a horseperson comes to understand and appreciate the cooperative nature of the horse, they begin winning with their horses.

Born to Communicate

There Is No Alpha in Natural Settings

Figure 7 All of the horses in a herd share leadership and surveillance. Each horse has a critical role, and many roles change through time.

There is no alpha in natural settings, but there are leaders, many leaders. If the mountain lion comes in from the west, and the lead mare is to the east, another horse leads the herd away from danger. All horses are taught by their herd to be a leader when leadership is needed to protect the herd. As well, all horses are taught by the herd to be followers, and it is this nature that allows the horse to be trained. Horses crave reliable leaders. To train a horse one must become the horse's leader. Leadership requires familiarity.

Unfortunately, many have been taught that they need to apply dominance theory to train a horse. Some have been instructed that to train a horse one must show the horse who is boss. Some trainers believe one can utilize dominance theory to force obedience and performance. If this was the case, one could force the horse to win the Kentucky Derby, right? Wrong. Willing partnerships win competitive events. The combination of horse and human can become something greater than the sum of man and horse, but only when the combination becomes mutually sympathetic. As you will see, in natural settings there is no alpha or fixed hierarchy. Leadership is shared and flexible, and agonistic behaviours are rare, and virtually never seen in the context of bullying.

In natural settings the horse's nature is one of communal survival. There is no alpha, but there are a variety of leaders. All horses in the harem are trained to lead and be led by all the others. This is the domestication sugar that allows horses to be trained by humans.

Born to Please

Training, Teaching and Learning the Language of Horses

Figure 8 Willing partnerships produce winning results. The pair bonded connection is a deep connection. Horses are born to please riders that know how to please horses. Familiarity facilitates connection. Accomplished horsefolk control the horse's feet with their mind and body. In many pursuits, the horse is the most qualified to make many of the decisions. A willing partnership allows duties to be shared, much as duties are shared in a herd.

Learning appropriate equitation science is best accomplished through behavioural and physiological understanding of the horse combined with extended periods of time spent with horses in diverse disciplines and cultures. In order to shape animal behaviour one must understand animal behaviour and learning science. Training is efficiently accomplished via facilitation of the horse's nature, rather than by force or coercion. Horses possess an inherent nature to appease not only other horses, but to appease the wishes of horsemen and horsewomen. Properly socialized horses readily accept human leadership. Horses are among the most efficient learners in the domestic animal kingdom.

The nature of the domestic horse is to pair with man willingly and to learn from him efficiently in exchange for security and comfort, important considerations for horses. When taught with respect and understanding, horses become safe and reliable. While force is not necessary to train horses, clear communication is. Horses learn best in the parasympathetic state. Training that puts the horse into the flight or sympathetic state generated by fear or pain and contained by ropes or pens is discouraged, unnecessary, and not in accordance with acceptable standards of animal appreciation and understanding. Training that exhausts the horse or creates prolonged fear in the horse intentionally, inflicts pain or severely restricts movement using force or rigs (physically restrictive devices) is inappropriate. Horses learn most effectively when taught using a language they understand and appreciate while relaxed and content. Troubled horses should be allowed to become untroubled before training resumes.

Trust and respect are established though familiarity and predictability. Timing and concision are necessary to train horses. Cues must blend with the rhythms and gaits of the horse. Accomplished horsefolk understand learning science, especially the scientific terms regarding teaching and training.

The primary component of all horsetraining is negative reinforcement. Negative reinforcement is utilized to operantly condition the horse to appropriately delivered cues. Pressure is carefully applied. The pressure is immediately released when the horse or foal gives the correct response, or approximates the correct response. Subsequent pressure and release shapes the behaviour.

Here is a basic example: Pressure is applied using the left rein. As the horse makes the first notion to the left, the pressure is released, conditioning a response to turn left when left rein pressure is applied. This training is done in a conscious fashion, and is therefore termed operant conditioning. So then; negative reinforcement is used to operantly condition horses.

Horses are trained with operant conditioning. Horses learn as humans learn. Humans are born with the wherewithal to teach horses, much as horses are born to teach horses. Horses have the ability to train people, and do. If a rider misuses spurs and the horse bucks the rider off in response to spur pressure, and then bucks him off again with the next spurring, the rider most often stops using the spurs to apply pressure. Horses are fast learners. Humans sometimes are not.

So then, pressure followed by release to the desired response is negative reinforcement. The process to teach the horse to turn left in this fashion is termed operant conditioning. Negative does not imply that the training method is unacceptable or insensitive to the horse. When properly applied and executed, negative reinforcement is the preferred humane method of training.

Mares teach their foals using negative reinforcement. If it is good enough for the mare, it is good enough for the human. The terms negative and positive have nothing to do with proper or improper methods when used in the context of training and teaching horses. Negative simply indicates that pressure applied in a timely concise fashion is subsequently taken away as the horse gives the correct response, or approximates the correct response. Successive successful pressures and releases shape and strengthen taught behaviours. The pressure needs to be applied with finesse. Separate behaviours can be chained together. Higher order cues can be added to the process. The cues are best applied at the correct stage of the horse's gait to achieve the correct response.

In behavioural learning terms, positive connotes adding something, such as a reward, as in positive reinforcement. Rubbing the horse after or during the correct response is an example. Positive punishment is applied with spurs, say, when the horse fails to respond correctly. Positive punishment, which can be unacceptable despite the terminology, is whacking the horse for giving the wrong response. While this method may have its place in horsemanship, the place is very small and infrequent. When the rider feels punishment is required to any given cue, the fault usually lies in the teaching and application of the cue by the rider, rather than by any fault of the horse. Horses learn exactly what they are taught, and many are mis-taught.

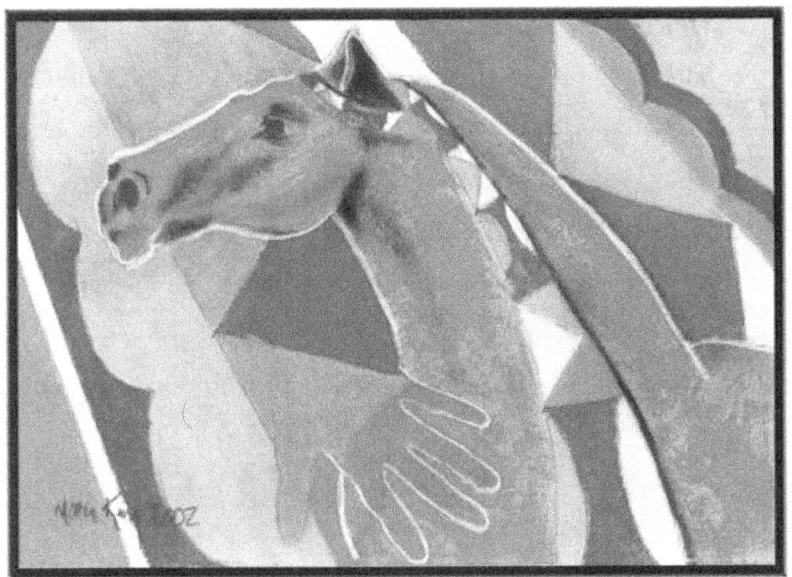

Figure 9 Painting by M King, Blackfeet artist. Courtesy of Riverbend Publishing

Positive reinforcement is adding something, such as food or a rubbing reward, while positive punishment is punishing a horse with painful actions.

Negative reinforcement can be enhanced with positive reinforcement. 1. The pressure is applied to the left as a timely and light tug on the left rein. 2. The horse correctly responds by turning left and the pressure is immediately released (this release is the reinforcement, the reinforcement is termed negative because pressure is taken away to reinforce the cue to turn left, thus the horse becomes operantly conditioned to turn left). 3. Once the pressure is released, or as the pressure is released, the horse can be rewarded with rubbing or verbal praise, which is using the addition of positive reinforcement to train.

Once the horse has responded to the pressure or cue, and the pressure is released, another something can be added to enhance the behaviour, to increase the likelihood of the behaviour repeating itself. This end act of reward, if utilized, is termed positive reinforcement. The release preceding the rub is the reinforcement that is termed negative. For those interested in understanding the principles of horsetraining and horsemanship, the terminology and concepts of learning science should be fully understood and appreciated.

4. If, after being asked to turn left, the horse turns to the right and bolts, it is often because the trainer has improperly or inadequately prepared the horse. In the case of the horse refusing to answer the cue, some trainers apply positive punishment, however inappropriate. Positive punishment would include painfully jerking the horse to the left with the reins, or spurring the right ribs to rectify the unwanted response.

Spurring or jerking the bit in the horse's mouth is scientifically termed positive punishment. Although termed positive punishment, this type of training (excessive or predominant use of punishment) can be dreadful for horses. Dread results in a fragile unreliable relationship with the rider. Remember this: the horse always has the last word. Always remember to make the training a good deal for the horse.

Willing partnerships are preferred to indentured servitude or forced behaviors. Fear of punishment is not a reliable training modality for the horse.

The combination of negative reinforcement accompanied by positive rewards is operant conditioning, sometimes called instrumental conditioning, and more commonly known as horsemanship.

The dam teaches the foal how to be a horse using a variety of these teaching techniques, as do humans when they train horses in later life. For a horse to be successfully trained by humans, the horse is best served to grow up to be a horse as taught by the mare. It is the mare and other horses that teach the foal to be a horse. Man has no role in teaching a foal to be a horse, as that is the mare's domain, and her herd's responsibility. Foals that grow up fully a horse as taught by the herd are the horses that are most willing to train.

Horsemanship is sharing sociality with the horse. Kinetic empathy is the shared method of communication. Kinetic empathy is the language of movement. Learn to train as the mare trains. Learn the kinetic empathy that is required to teach horses. Let the mare initially train the foal, please. The foal will then become a horse that has the principles of learning embedded in her psyche. The horse will become trainable.

Horses are horses. Folk are folk. They live together, sharing a social fabric. Horses and horsefolk possess many similar aspects of living, including extensive sociality, communication and learning.

Enjoy your horses. Listen to them. Absorb their language. Make their language your language. Blend into their society.

Born to Friend

Domestication Illuminated

To grasp how man and horse societies may have merged long ago is to appreciate the contemporary horse/rider relationship. To develop positive relationships with the horse, one must come into an awareness of the long evolved social nature of horses. Horsemanship merges human nature with the nature of the horse. The language of horsemanship allows horses and humans to achieve pairings that achieve far greater accomplishments than the sum of horse and rider would allow.

The social nature of horses is one of constant awareness. Constant awareness is essential for group survival. The horseperson is best served to blend into the survival construct of the horse to achieve willing partnerships. Willing partnerships form the basis of the cooperative survival construct of the horse. Cooperative partnerships facilitate survival of horse and rider. Horses know to work together with other horses—provided they were taught to be a horse by other horses (appropriate socialization)—and can be taught to work together with a rider.

Horses living in harems in natural settings remain constantly aware of all the other horses in the herd. Survival behaviours are learned and taught within the herd. Socialization teaches survival behaviours to growing horses. Mankind capitalizes on the horse's survival behaviours to train and pair with horses. Successful horsetrainers train horses as the mare trains the foal. Horses are all about learning and awareness. Horses are born to learn. Horses are born to be aware of others to facilitate their learning. Horses learn to be horses from the mare and herd. The learning and teaching principles applied in horsetraining are the principles established in the herd.

Awareness is essential for learning, and also for surveillance.

Except for brief spells of sleep and play, horses constantly observe their surroundings for any unwelcome developments, such as the approach of predators. Predators include anything with which the horse is unfamiliar. All unfamiliar creatures, places, and things are considered suspect and possible dangers. Neophobia is the term used to describe this survival trait.

Most horses are innately fearful of all new things. This is normal and expected behaviour. Horses constantly survey their surroundings with their stellar vision. They see by day or night, and nearly 360°. Eyes set high in their head, horses graze and gaze, they watch. The grazing, nipping, and chewing motion rotates their head enough to see behind them on a periodic basis. When not grazing or dozing, horses focus on watching. When dozing or sleeping, others horses watch for them. All horses need other horses for behavioural health. Foals raised by the mare and herd in a grazing setting develop into easily trainable animals. As to competitive pursuit, it is the herd of mares and foals that teaches thoroughbreds and other breeds to run at speed in close company. Playing cohorts give growing horses the confidence to run with, through, and by other horses in all-out gallops about the pasture.

Horses learn how to move from other horses. They learn how to see and to graze, and perhaps most importantly, how to effectively communicate with others. For a horse to effectively grow up to communicate with humans, the foal must first be taught the communication skills to communicate with other horses. This is the essence of socialization. Appropriate socialization within the herd develops normal equine behaviour. If we want our horses to grow up to be normal and trainable, they must grow up under the tutelage of the mare and herd. Orphaned foals raised by humans do not grow up to learn normally, as many have discovered. When foals are orphaned, it is essential that other horses become their teachers at some point during the development.

Imprint training during the first hours and days of life interferes with normal development. While familiarity with humans during this phase can be productive, training is often counterproductive. We know imprint training is not necessary to train horses, and it is here that humans need to follow the medical principle of "first, do no harm." Imprint training can cause irreparable behavioural harm.

Born to Play

Play and sparring are prevalent in the horse behavioural profile in natural settings. Play develops the expressions of movement horses require for behavioural health and prosperity.

If your horses are not playing each day, expect your horse to partake in certain activities you do not consider playful.

The equid ethogram is the endless list of natural behaviours and behaviour patterns of horses observed in natural settings. Cribbing is not in the ethogram observed in natural settings, so we all know who is at fault when a horse develops into a cribber.

Horsefolk need to make sure horses are afforded adequate and fulfilling play, most desirably with other horses, but also with horsefolk. Play and socialization provide activities that hone agility and promote the development of strong and durable musculoskeletal systems.

Riding can be play to a horse. I have often observed play in natural settings, and am happy to have confirmed that there is a riding component to equid play in the equid ethogram. For those who might feel riding is something a bit alien to a horse, it may well be to horses who are not adequately socialized in a harem type setting with conspecifics of both sexes. Horses who grow up in herd settings become acclimated to having other horses "ride" them. From the side, young horses are often noted to put their front legs over the back of their playmates. As well, the jaw and neck are often rested on the backs of other horses. All of this playful activity initially habituates horses to having another creature on their back. When riding time arrives, pressure on their back is not completely foreign when it becomes time for the human to hop aboard.

Horses are additionally habituated and desensitized to having someone on their back in the training process. Those horses who never had the experience of others applying pressure to their backs are more reluctant to become desensitized, and sometimes take longer to train to safely board without inciting flight or bucking.

If you watch foals and yearlings in herd settings, you will see them applying various pressures to the backs of one another. The more horses become comfortable with others on their backs, the better. Socialization is critical to a future of wholesome health, both physical and behavioural.

Socialization scenarios in which foals and conspecifics are allowed to play, ride, and spar offer many advantages. These horses know how to learn. They know how to run in close company with others.

I cannot stress socialization enough in the development of horses. Socialization is essential for future health, learning, and healing. It is the unsocialized horse that is prone to injury and untrainability. Unsocialized horses often become untrainable, and later unwanted, and we know where that leads.

Socialization is important so that horses do not become unwanted later in life, as it is most often the unsocialized horse that becomes the unwanted horse. Socialization strengthens the growing horse, bestowing the horse with well-developed behaviour, joints, and bones as a result of all the locomotion and play with others.

Born to Mingle

Grooming

Figure 10 Grooming, massage, and daily hands-on inspections create connection and familiarity between horse and human. Stabled horses require at least an hour of daily massage each day to maintain their social need for touch with others. A daily massage allows a daily examination. Horses that are stabled require a thorough health exam by their guardians each morning. Forage needs to be available ad libitum (according to pleasure). The total ration needs to be formulated and balanced according to the horses age, use, and temperament. The horse is a trickle feeder, requiring the forage portion of the diet to be provided on a constant basis. Locomotion is an essential ingredient of proper nutrition.

To pair bond and establish familiarity, one must rub their

horse, often and regular. Massage is essential to support the health of stabled horses; full body massages each and every day, please. A massage each day keeps the vets at bay. Massage is both therapeutic and diagnostic. People who rub their horses, know their horses. They know the legs and hooves. They find the aches and pains before the aches become strains. Rub your stabled horses, please, rub them everywhere, do not forget to rub the coronary bands. Rub them before tacking up; rub to make sure they are sound. Rub, rub, and rub some more, as rubbing creates winners. Forget the Bute, and rub. Horses in herds rub one another extensively and regularly. If you are your horse's herdmate, you best rub.

Brushing and grooming stimulate digestive and circulatory functions. The grooming process allows bonding between horse and human. Brushing enhances nutrition, circulation, and many other physiological functions. If you are confused about rubbing, watch horses rub one another and watch horses rub themselves. Emulate how horses rub one another.

Stalled horses need a good hour or two of brushing and rubbing a day to know the enrichment they would receive in a herd. I have seen people train horses to ride by simply brushing them everywhere everyday for days on end. Brushing can involve and incorporate pressure and release and reward, creating the establishment of cues, boundaries, and yields. Mutual beneficence is the result. Both horse and human benefit.

Brushing.

This little neighbor girl watched my foal born decades back. After the baby had been taught to be a horse by the mare and subsequently weaned, the girl returned. She came to me and explained that since the mare had finished teaching the foal, she wanted her turn to teach the yearling. I smiled and said okay. I had trained the babe to halter and habituated him to horsefolk when he was three or four months old.

Each day the little girl came and brushed Nate. Brushing, brushing, brushing. Pressure and release taught the yearling to yield to her properly applied pressure. One day I looked up, and my little horse-brusher was riding around the pasture bareback with a halter. I have witnessed a variety of American Indian children teach their horses in this fashion. The constant rubbing and brushing allowed an intimate familiarity to develop between the horse and child. Familiarity allows pair bonding, and pair bonding allows training. This is the science. Training without a glimmer of dominance.

When a horse becomes troubled, stop the training and brush and rub, please.

Troubled horses do not learn, while brushed horses learn well. To brush your horse is to train your horse. Forget about showing your horse who is boss, show your horse who cares about her.

Brush your stabled horses, often, please. Rub and brush. Walk them. Hand graze them. Keep them moving. Lunge them. The word lunge comes from lung, it seems, and if it doesn't, it should.

To walk and lunge your stabled horses on a daily basis is to enhance and maintain pulmonary health. The key to prevent bleeding (EIPH) in racehorses is abundant daily locomotion beyond the training regimen. Abundant daily locomotion enhances lung health and resilience. Bleeding during a race is best prevented by miles of daily walking between races.

For horses, to move is to breathe, and to breathe is to move. Abundant daily walking also prevents the development of Chronic Obstructive Pulmonary Disease, or heaves. Make sure your barns are well-ventilated. Horses evolved to breathe clean air, and cannot handle dirty air like people sometimes can.

Notice how often horses self-groom their lower legs. Rub the legs all up and down before tacking up. Flex all the joints, please. Get the digital pulse, por favor. Find any tender areas before the areas become problematic, and the horse becomes lame.

Remember to rub your horse's fetlocks, pasterns, and coronets with your bare hands before and after riding each day. To know your horse, rub your horse everywhere every day.

Rubbing simulates movement. If you cannot provide adequate daily locomotion, you best get in there and rub.

Stall-rested horses need massaged and passively flexed for at least two hours a day to maintain health.

Friends, forage, locomotion, and rubbing.

Get in touch with your horses with your hands.

Figure 11 The author in Kentucky, where he testified before the Kentucky Horse Racing Commission to support the health and welfare of racehorses.

Born to Move

Every aspect of horse health is dependent on locomotion, my friends, yet this deepest nature of the horse is often restricted. Stabled horses require miles and hours of daily walking to maintain both physical and behavioural health. Keep your horses moving for optimal health. Whenever you see horses standing about all day, expect illness and veterinarians to arrive. Deprivations of movement and locomotion are the cause of the majority of health problems in horses. When horses are stabled, they need to be walked miles each day to keep the veterinarian away.

Get creative with locomotion. Place your feeders so the horses have to move about to eat. Movement is the essence of the horse. Keep your horses moving, moving to keep them warm and healthy. Digestion is dependent on locomotion. Stabled horses require miles of walking each and every day to maintain optimal health. Humans most often fail their horses by depriving them of the abundant locomotion they require to stay healthy each and every day. Every system of the horse is dependent on abundant daily locomotion.

To keep warm in cold weather horses require appropriate and constant forage 24/7, friends, and abundant movement. Shelter is always nice, provided the air remains fresh and pure and never is dusty or full of particulates. Sheltering is often responsible for the development of heaves, so find a balance for your horses, my friends.

Whenever you see horses standing around in the same place all day, expect trouble, veterinary bills, as well as hoof, digestive, training, respiratory, and metabolic trouble. Stalled or corralled horses need to move miles everyday, so saddle up, folks, and get your horses moving. To move is to thrive if you are a horse.

Born to Graze

Abundant locomotion and foraging are essential natures of the horse.

Locomotion and fiber ingestion are the essences of horse health. The forage has to be appropriate low-energy forage for maintenance. In natural settings, horses never fast for over three hours, and most seldom fast for over one hour. Horses are trickle feeders, moving, grazing, and communing while watching their world with the keenest vision, smell, taste, hearing, and feel on the planet. Horses can see by day or night. They utilize their vibrissae and lips to feel through the forage they ingest.

Horses in natural settings eat two thirds of the time, walking and grazing together. The key to keeping confined horses healthy is to re-create an abundant movement scenario in the stable.

Horses locked down in a stall each day are the horses that become sick. When stabling is necessary, the horses have to brought out of their stalls several times each day and moved about. In addition to training and riding regimens, the horses need walking for at least a few hours each day. Forage deprivation is the cause of most stereotypies. Forage deprivation combined with deprivations of locomotion and socialization are responsible for the vast majority of ill health in horses. Everything goes back to providing appropriate friends, forage, and locomotion.

Empty stomachs in stabled horses are cause for much trouble. Horses should seldom be without a bite of forage. Forage deprivation causes a wide variety of horse pathologies. The forage has to appropriate for the condition and use of the horse. Rations need to be appropriately and constantly balanced.

By now we all know what failing to provide these simple roughage and stomach-content requirements causes in horses (poor learning ability, stereotypies, lack of motivation to perform, lameness, tying -up, ulcers, more veterinary bills...)

Oh, and do not forget water. And where the water is placed. Fresh water is required at all times, and in a location where each horse can drink comfortably, preferably with the open view.

Remember horses' good and essential friend, salt. Lead a horse to salt and she will lick and later drink. Make sure salt always travels with your horse. It seems lack of salt while traveling causes a lack of hydration, which leads to colic. Horses require salt and water 24/7, just as they do forage and locomotion.

Forage balancers are often required. Calcium and phosphorus make up bone, and bone makes a horse durable and sound. Do not forget the bone minerals, please. Balance your horse's nutrition correctly. Feed your horse like a horse would feed in natural settings.

Healthy horses make happy and willing partners.

When we have problems with a horse, we all know to first make sure that the forage, friends, and locomotion are adequate, plentiful, and appropriate before devising behavioural modification strategies that overlook these essentials. Unhappy horses are hard to train, as are horses who do not become pairbonded to their trainer.

When confronted with a horse with behaviour or training issues, we have all learned to *first* consider stabling as a primary factor in teaching, learning, and training. The proper method to address training issues is to first address stabling and socialization issues.

Locomotion is also essential for pulmonary health. Horses locked down all day bleed into their lungs when exercised strenuously, as in a race. The cause of pulmonary bleeding in racehorses is clearly a lack of abundant daily locomotion. In addition to the training regimens, stabled horses require miles of daily walking to maintain the health of all systems. This aspect of the nature of the horse (movement) is the most overlooked aspect of husbandry. For horses, to move is to breathe, and to breathe is to move.

Metabolic disease and laminitis are caused by a lack of adequate locomotion. Colic is caused by a lack of locomotion. Obesity is caused by a lack of locomotion. Tying up is caused by a lack of locomotion. Bucking is caused by a lack of locomotion. Cribbing is caused by a lack of locomotion and deprivations of chewing and grazing. Horses evolved to chew 80 times a minute for 16 to 20 hours a day. Anything less is cause for the development of physical and behavioural pathologies.

Keep your horses happy with friends, forage, socialization, and locomotion. A five-mile walk a day keeps the veterinarian away. Hand walking or bareback riding at a walk for a few hours each day are required to maintain the health of stabled horses.

Stalled horses require movement. For horses unable to move because of injury, we must re-create movement with massage and passive flexion of all the limbs. Horses require friends, forage, and locomotion on a near constant basis to maintain behavioural and performance health.

Born to Heal

Restorative healing in Equus caballus

Restoration strategies that recreate the horse's social grazing preferences facilitate and potentiate horse healing. Appropriate healing of many equine maladies is encouraged when the veterinarian provides appropriate initial treatment and subsequently carefully facilitates a scenario to provide the horse with abundant forage, friendship, and locomotion.

Grazing pasture in an open setting with other horses, when appropriately orchestrated, has the potential to provide the most profound and often the most cost-effective healing of musculoskeletal infirmities and injuries. For conditions allowed to progress to lameness, time is required, often months. When musculoskeletal conditions are detected early, before lameness ensues, short-term rest and restorative strategies encourage solid healing (days to weeks). Both long and short term healing are enhanced when the horse is content with the forage, friendship, and locomotion resources. Avoid unnecessary restrictions to locomotion whenever feasible.

The earlier inflammation is detected, the shorter the time period is required to heal. Healing in a social-grazing setting is a long-evolved trait of the horse. Horses acclimated to herd and pasture settings during their development respond best to restorative healing.

Horsefolk need to take special care not to exceed the horse's adaptability regarding stabling and healing.

Horses require a sense of comfort and security for physical and mental restoration (and maintenance). An adequate social grazing environment, or appropriate facsimile thereof, often provides the most comfort to the most horses. Horses provided with adequate socialization throughout their upbringing are most responsive to these strategies. For horses, comfort and security come from friendship, forage, and, most-critically, a near-constant casual locomotion. Young horses and newborns learn to be horses from the dam and herd, and foals are best served to develop with horses in an appropriate grazing environment, as well. Horses learn to socialize, communicate, graze, locomote, run at speed in close company, play, smell, balance, move, and compete from their mother along with the herd members.

Corral or stall rest is counterproductive to healing, as it deprives horses of all three healing essentials. Horses heal efficiently in a social grazing setting, not one of isolation and deprivation. To a horse, restoration, from the word rest, ideally implies grazing open country in a herd setting with abundant environmental resources; appropriate grasslands to graze and walk, salt, and appropriately placed clean water. The properly managed social grazing setting with the open view is the environment in which horses evolved to thrive and heal.

Healthy physical and mental developments are best actualized in a social grazing environment. Neonates rely on their dam for critical early learning processes, including sensual development, locomotion, and early mobility. The development of agility, coordination and athleticism in early life is critical to subsequent mental health and soundness. Abundant social contact, grooming, sleep, play, athletic development, and social bonding occur during early herd life. Horses rely on constant contact and frequent interactions with other horses for healthy mental and physical development.

Opportunities for the abundant expression of normal equine behaviour and *motion* promote healing.

Unfortunately, healing opportunities of this sort are not available everywhere, especially in the more urban equestrian settings. Space and grazing limitations restrict healing opportunities. In these scenarios, the horse's preferences have to recreated with carefully designed and implemented ENRICHMENT strategies that provide some fashion of near constant forage ingestion that allow oral and physical and movement and motion. Stabling scenarios often restrict social expression and sensual contact. Horses are sensitive to these deprivations, which result in stress, which complicates and delays healing.

LOCOMOTION is essential for both horse health and healing.

Husbandry, healing, and rehabilitation nearly always benefit from appropriately managed and free choice locomotion strategies that are constantly tailored to the horse's healing process. Locomotion is required not only for normal healing, but for normal digestion, respiration, hoof health, circulation, and all other physiologic functions of the horse. Stall rest is at the expense of many systems, especially the hoof and metabolic systems. Digestion and respiration are compromised by confinement and restriction of movement. Metabolic, digestive, circulatory, hoof health, musculoskeletal, and nervous, systems, as well as the all other systems and functions of the horse, are dependent upon adequate and appropriate locomotion for normal functioning and/or healing.

For horses that are hospitalized, paddocked, stabled, and corralled active implementation and re-creation of the social pasture setting is necessary to maintain health and promote healing. The absence of abundant forage, friends, and locomotion are detrimental to a stabled or hospitalized horse's health, if not welfare. Medical conditions are apt to deteriorate in the face of the deprivations created by stabling and hospitalization.

Stalled horses heal poorly. Locomotion, social, and forage deprivations create problems for horses. In addition to appropriate medical treatment, veterinarians and stable managers must creatively provide horses with abundant socialization, forage, and locomotion to maintain health and facilitate healing.

Horses also heal horsefolk, and those horsefolk that implement these healing strategies often experience a sense of healing themselves, it seems. The human/horse bond runs deep. Domestication of the horse is a co-evolving evolutionary process. The human perspective is being shaped by the horse's perspective these days. Appreciation of the science of equine behaviour and equitation is a welcome change for the horse after centuries of considerable subjugation.

Born to Run

Appreciating Horses

In consideration of the horse's nature and behaviour, horsewomen and horsemen are obligated to provide horses an appropriate environment, unhindered neonatal development, formation and fulfillment of the mare-foal bond, adequate nutrition, sufficient sociobehavioural circumstances and training and horsemanship modalities based on the horse's innate perspectives and sensitivities.

By nature the horse is a precocious grazer of the plains, a social and herd animal, and flighty. Horsemanship and training are best accomplished through behavioural appreciation of the horse and facilitation of the horse's nature, rather than by force or coercion. Horses are best trained in a relaxed, calm state. Training that puts the horse into the flight or sympathetic state generated by fear and punishment while restricted by rigs or round pens is discouraged, and not in accordance with acceptable standards of animal training. Horsetraining and horse teaching methods are best based on scientific studies regarding the nature of the horse. Horses learn preferentially in a relaxed state from a calm experienced handler with adept communication skills.

Social behaviour in natural feral settings is the 'natural' behaviour that 'natural' horsemanship utilizes to appreciate the nature of the horse.

As to dominance, the science reveals that free-ranging horses form social hierarchies that are complex and rarely linear. Under natural open range conditions with adequate resources, horses seldom have the equivalent of an alpha individual because the roles of leadership and defense are more critical than domination. Dominance theory as a training modality is not only discouraged, but also appears inappropriate. The formation of order in horse groups sustains collective welfare and enhances group survival, and reflects leadership rather than domination. It is important veterinarians and students of equine behaviour appreciate this science.

There is no alpha. Leadership is shared and alternated and variable and context dependent in established harems in natural settings. Dominance is rare, and certainly not prevalent. When present at all, it facilitates group protection and stability. Horses share leadership. Survival is herd based, rather than individual based. The lead mare leads the horses to water and grazing and resting places. She drinks first to make sure the water is safe, rather than because she dominates the others. Students of equine behaviour appreciate shared leadership and herd stability. Horses seek competent leadership and are willing to accept competent leadership from humans.

The horse is special in retaining the ability to thrive in feral conditions independent of man. This allows us to study their true nature versus their stable nature and to apply that knowledge to their welfare as it pertains to training.

Horse retains the ability to survive without us, and survive well.

It behooves humankind to take care with horses. Sensitive horsefolk respect the 60 million year development of the horse's social behaviour and development. They appreciate equine intelligence in regard to both training and husbandry, and what the future might hold.

Stabling is unnatural. Horses graze and walk together 60-70% of the time under natural circumstances, eating and moving from spot to spot independently but within a few meters of the next horse. Stable managers and horse owners should make every effort to accommodate or recreate these long-evolved herd grazing and life-in-motion preferences for proper physiological function and mental health.

Horses require other horses for proper health and prosperity. Horses prefer the constant companionship of other horses. A horse should seldom be kept alone. Horses being mixed with other horses and expected to share resources should be properly acclimated socially, and be given the required space to adjust to new herds without injury or undue stress. Every effort should be made to provide horses with the social benefit of appropriate companion horses through times of stress and illness.

Horsewomen and men need to appreciate the sensual nature of the horse, and understand the physiological needs of the horse. Horses prefer the open view. If they cannot be in physical contact with other horses, they need to see and smell other horses for proper behavioural functioning and responsiveness.

Water is the most important nutrient, and must be provided in consideration of equine behavioural preferences. Salt is the most important mineral, and should be provided daily in some fashion.

Grazing is the preferred and predominant equine activity. Horses did not evolve to metabolize grains and non-structured carbohydrates, or to remain stationary for even short periods of time. Serious metabolic issues develop when horses become sedentary grain eaters, and this lifestyle should not be imposed on horses.

Play and sleep are naturally occurring preferences that require accommodation however horses are housed or stabled, as deprivation results in behavioural deterioration.

Horses are physiologically dependent on shared social grooming and sensual contact companionship. If stabling precludes these preferences from fulfillment, then every effort need be applied to replace or recreate these needs on a daily basis.

These behavioural considerations apply to horses in transport, and for those horses, however unwanted, man is obligated to provide the proper environment, social functioning, nutrition, medical care, and exercise to sufficiently assure health and comfort during travel.

As to performance, every care and precaution need be taken to avoid exceeding the adaptability of the horse. All of the horse's normal natural sensation should remain fully intact and functional without undue pharmaceutical influence. The horse's metabolic, physical, medical, and behavioural limitations are best monitored by equine veterinary professionals on an intense comprehensive basis.

Professional veterinary societies and organizations are encouraged to provide education regarding equine behaviour.

Equine Behaviour and the Practice of Veterinary Medicine

Abstract:
Review of The Application of Equine Behavior to the Practice of Veterinary Medicine is a presentation of the current behavioral science regarding the health and healing of the horse. The review is a behavior primer describing the essential behavioral approaches required to fulfill the inherent natures of the horse to facilitate optimal equine health and healing. Fulfilling the inherent requisite needs of horses from the horse perspective, rather than from the human perspective, enhances equine welfare and prosperity. Medical application of the evolved nature of horses expands the

veterinarian's ability to successfully heal horses and create preventive health protocols.

Horses began their journey through time 60 million years ago. Three million years ago the footsteps of humans were fossilized next to the hoofprints of horses, suggesting that humans have been contemplating horses for some time. But it was not until perhaps ten thousand years ago that human societies began the dance of domestication with the horse. Over thousands of years, perhaps tens of thousands of years, the horse herds gradually merged with human societies. A shared language described by contemporary scientists as kinetic empathy, a language of movement, and similar compatible social structures facilitated the merging of the two species.

There is archeological evidence that humans had formed an intimate and intermingled relationship with horses by 5500 years ago in Botai, where the horsefolk stabled and milked horses, and probably rode them. Horses provided these early horsefolk with much of the essentials they needed for group survival. It is interesting to note that large domestic dogs lived with these early horsefolk as well, but no other domestic animals. To understand the domestication process is to enhance our appreciation of equine behaviour. Horses became domesticated because they found a niche with people thousands of years ago on the steppes of Kazakhstan. Both trained and wild horses existed in this realm south of Russia and west of China. A population of horses more amenable to captivity and taming than their wild counterparts provided the stock for the first horse societies. Rather than plucking wild horses out of the wild and taming them, it is thought that over tens of thousands of years a relationship developed in a shared niche, drawing the two social species together.

By the early 20th century the closest living relative to *Equus caballus*, the Tarpan, had gone extinct. No truly wild horses remain. All of today's caballine horses are descended from an original, and possibly separate, population of horses that were amenable to being tamed and selectively bred by humans. It appears to have taken tens of thousands of years to fully domesticate the horse, and to eventually attain control of breeding. Breeding initially consisted primarily of selection for docility and amenability to captivity, and later milking, riding, driving, and stabling. In contemporary culture, selective breeding often involves selecting for the best athlete, or attempting to select for the best athlete. In addition to genetics, this presentation will focus on the socialization aspect of raising horses, and portray the importance of nurture on the eventual behavioral and physical health of the adult athlete.

No longer does human society depend on horse society for survival as it once did. Although still bred for trainability, more and more horses are today bred for specific performance goals. These days, horses provide people with entertainment, recreation, sport, esteem, performance, and pleasure, and, as ever, but in fewer and fewer reaches, utility. Other than stockfolk, few others rely on horses to sustain a pastoral livelihood. This new role of the horse requires renewed studies and considerations of equine behavior.

Horsefolk and veterinarians alike remain enticed and intrigued by horses. The science of equine behaviour attempts to appreciate just who horses are, and from the horse perspective. To appreciate the horse perspective, behaviourists explore the evolution and domestication of the horse. We continue to find ourselves attempting to appreciate how the current human/horse relationship came to be so as to facilitate a smooth trouble free relationship with our horses. As well, appropriate breeding, socialization, and training of horses helps minimize behavioural wastage. Behavioral wastage is responsible for well over half of the unwanted horses in modern societies across the globe.

To understand where our relationship with the horse is headed, veterinary behaviour practitioners attempt to see where the human/horse relationship has been, and to subsequently help modify and refine the relationship to favor the horse. Humans continue to live with horses and continue to learn from them, as all horsefolk have through time. When horse and man coexisted together shoulder to shoulder day after day, a sophisticated understanding of the other developed. Today, much less time is spent learning from horses. Contemporary practitioners must research and make themselves aware of the behavioural principles that were once gleaned from a near-constant exposure to horses through all stages of their development. We study the evolution and domestication of the horse to better help us appreciate the horses we have in our hands today. Evolution and domestication provide a basis for the understanding of equine behaviour. Man has attempted to refine his relationship with the horse ever since the first kid grabbed a mane and swung atop a horse. To become a partner with the flighty, powerful (but trainable and tamable) grazer of the plains remains the goal.

Fulfillment of all of our caballine horses' evolved needs promotes optimum health and soundness, and subsequently optimum performance. A horse cannot be coerced to win the

Kentucky Derby. The people must work with the horse, fulfilling the horse's requirements for vigor. If we understand equine behaviour, we understand what makes horses do our bidding, and do it willingly and well. To this day, horses seek to appease their domesticators much as they appease others in horse societies and herds. Horses are willing learners. This learning behavior is a result of evolutionary development of a complex social lifestyle.

The productivity of horses is dependent upon social development. Appropriate socialization with other horses in a herd setting best prepares horses to be subsequently trained by horsefolk. Pastured horses train up and learn more efficiently than stabled horses, as it is the herd that teaches learning skills to the growing horse. Appropriate, efficient, and considerate training of horses is predicated by their previous socialization by the dam and other horses. Trainability is heavily influenced by the intensity and type of stabling and husbandry, and the type of training. In the latest revolution of horsemanship, the area of appropriate socialization and stabling has not received the attention it deserves.

Horses are a quiet species. They prefer calm, and learn most efficiently in tranquil, familiar settings. Horses must know and be comfortable and secure in their environment to be able to learn as horsefolk hope them to learn. Horsefolk all know what we want from our horses, however in this paper I shall present the science of what our horses want and need from humans, the science of equine behaviour. Equine behaviour is not only the basis of training and trainability, but also the very basis of equine health. To succeed in our endeavors with horses (whatever the our equine goals or pursuits), our horses are best served to receive what they preferentially need and require behaviourally, nutritionally, socially, physically, environmentally, visually, and metabolically. In order to properly care for horses and successfully teach and train horses, horsefolk must know horses. They must know who the gregarious grazers of the plains are. They must know how to properly socialize horses through their growth phase to ensure that their horses grow up to be horses. Horses raised out of the herd context are vulnerable to behavioural insecurities later in life. Most behavioural wastage is due to improper socialization and husbandry.

Rather than being dissimilar to us, horses are much like us. In this presentation, I attempt to clarify humankind's social and communicative similarities to horses. As with people, strong social bonds develop between individual horses and groups of horses. This herd nature results in intense social pair and herd bonds. Horses need other horses. Horses require other horses for security, comfort, and behavioural health. Horses need friends throughout their entire life, first their teaching mother, and then their teaching herd. Today's domestic horse needs horse friends and human friends, although horses do retain the wherewithal to survive just fine without horsefolk. Horses need friends so greatly and constantly, that horses allow horsefolk to substitute as friends. This is possible because man shares a sociality with domestic horses. We speak their gesture language, and horses speak ours. We share a language of movement, and language described as kinetic empathy.

Domestic horse is no longer human prey, and has not been for thousands of years. Horse has been brought into the circle of humanity, along with a dozen or so other domesticates that share an adequate sociality with mankind to be allowed to develop a mutually beneficial relationship.

Horse and man have co-evolved together for thousands, if not tens of thousands of years. Each knows the other, well, and horses have proven to know the nature of people more consistently than people know the nature of horses. It is paramount that horsefolk appreciate the social and communicative nature of horses, and deal with horses in a fashion that is appropriate to their long-evolved social nature.

In addition to adequate and appropriate sociality and socialization, the importance of the need for near-constant motion is paramount to equine behavioral and physical health. Locomotion is essential for horse health. In natural settings, horses move about grazing, playing, trekking, and variety of other movements as much a two-thirds of the time. Abundant movement provides constant connection and communication with the other horses in the herd, and as well, sustains the overall and physiologic functions of the horse. Plentiful locomotor activity facilitates behavioural expression and maintains physiologic health. An essential interdependence exists between horse health and locomotion.

Horses evolved to be near-constant walkers and grazers. Horses did not evolve to be confined. Pulmonary health and resilience are dependent on miles of daily walking. For a horse, to breathe is to move, and to move is to breathe. Sedentary husbandry results in pulmonary deterioration. In addition to conditioning regimens, equine athletes require miles of additional walking each and every day. Horses are born to move on a near constant basis, and move they must. Horses deprived of movement develop stereotypies to simulate the movement they need. Jaw movement is critical to establish normal digestion. In natural settings, horses move and graze 16-20 hours a day. They chew 70-

90 times a minute for most of the day. If this essential digestive is not fulfilled in the stable, cribbing, weaving, and colic emerge.

Despite domestication and selective breeding for docility and captivity, horse health remains dependent on locomotion. Locomotion is inherent to every aspect of equine health. Locomotion is essential for normal digestion. Hours of abundant daily locomotion are required to maintain respiratory and metabolic functions. Hoof, bone, tendon, ligament, muscle, joint and behavioral health are dependent on hours of daily walking and socializing. If horses are not allowed to move about freely and socialize with other familiar horses grazing and chewing as they evolved to do, they become metabolically vulnerable and behaviorally troubled. Horses deprived of locomotion and constant forage ingestion develop strategies to maintain the motion and oral security they feel they need to survive. When horses are deprived of adequate locomotion and foraging, they develop strategies to maintain body and jaw movement. Movement is the essential nature of the horse. Horses deprived of friends, forage, and locomotion are at risk to develop stereotypies to provide themselves with the movement they need to survive. As well, deprived horses become vulnerable to colic, metabolic disease, laminitis, lameness, and pulmonary diseases. Chronic obstructive pulmonary disease and exercise induced pulmonary hemorrhage are exacerbated by deprivations of locomotion.

The primary premise of equine behavioural health is this: in natural settings, horses walk and graze with other horses two thirds of the time. They take a step and graze, then another step or two grazing and moving along, always observing their surroundings, grazing while in touch with other members of the herd unless playing, occasionally dozing or sleeping under the secure and established watch of others. Horses that are not afforded the opportunity to graze and walk much of the time take up with behaviours to replicate essential locomotion.

Horses require friends, forage, and locomotion to stay healthy and productive. These needs are required to be re-created in the stable. Horses need clean air and abundant movement for normal athletic respiratory function. In rural pasture settings, these requirements are easy to fulfill. In the stabled, extensive efforts are required to re-create and fulfill the horse's inherent needs. Open grasslands and steppes are the geography and environs from where the most recent predecessors of *Equus caballus* evolved. The further we remove horses from their social-grazer-of-the-plains inclinations, the more deleterious health issues develop, requiring treatment and management by veterinarians. Failing to fulfill the horses needs often results in therapeutic failures, so it behooves veterinarians to ensure the husbandry is adequate.

Stabling, stalling, hospitalization and transport all deprive horses of their preferences for friends, forage, and locomotion. Although convenient for horsefolk and veterinarians, stabling is inconvenient for horses. Stabling limits the resources of friends, forage, and locomotion. Stabling creates bad air, and allows pathogens and parasites to travel easily between horses. When hospitalization is required, mending horses are best served to have their natural needs re-created abundantly. The air must be kept clean, and forage must be always available. Opportunities for movement and simulation of grazing with friends must be provided in abundance. Once our horses' behavioural needs are understood, appreciated, and fulfilled, the learning and training can advance. Enrichment strategies re-create the needs of stabled horses. Those strategies that best replicate the grazer of the plains scenario promote the best health, learning, and performance from horses. When stall rest is indicated, passive flexion, massage, and variety of other physical therapies should be instituted. If horses cannot move, their caretakers must replace the movement with extensive physical therapy.

Locomotion and socialization are essential for both horse health and healing. Husbandry, healing, and rehabilitation nearly always benefit from appropriately managed locomotion strategies that are constantly tailored to the horse's healing process. Locomotion is required not only for normal healing, but for normal digestion, respiration, hoof health, circulation, and all other physiologic functions of the horse. Stall rest is at the expense of many systems, especially the hoof and metabolic systems. Digestion and respiration are compromised by confinement and restriction of movement. Metabolic, digestive, circulatory, hoof health, musculoskeletal, and nervous, systems, as well as the all other systems and functions of the horse, are dependent upon adequate and appropriate locomotion for normal functioning and/or healing.

For horses that are hospitalized, paddocked, stabled, and corralled active implementation and re-creation of the social pasture setting is required to optimize and maintain health and promote healing. Medical conditions are apt to deteriorate in the face of the deprivations of forage, friends, and locomotion. Re-creation of a natural setting in the stall is the biggest challenge veterinarians and caretakers face in maintaining the health of hospitalized or stabled horses.

In addition to appropriate medical treatment, veterinarians and stable managers must creatively provide horses with abundant socialization, forage, and locomotion to maintain health and facilitate healing within the parameters of acceptable medical and surgical treatment. Restriction of locomotion to facilitate healing necessitates the implementation of enrichment strategies to simulate locomotion, including massage, passive flexion, and a wide variety of physical therapies.

Horses also heal horsefolk, and those horsefolk that implement these healing strategies often experience a sense of healing themselves, it seems. The human/horse bond runs deep. Domestication of the horse is a co-evolving evolutionary process. The human perspective is being shaped by the horse's perspective these days. Appreciation of the science of equine behavior and equitation is encouraged to support the renewed interest in equine medicine and welfare, and to facilitate the veterinarian's role of providing horses with their essential needs.

References

Chyoke A, Olsen S & Grant S 2006 *Horses and Humans, The Evolution of Human-Equine Relationships*, BAR International Series 1560, Archeopress, England, ISBN 1 84171 990 0

Gustafson S, DVM, *a Contemporary Approach to Equine Behavior Education*, 2011 World Veterinary Congress Proceedings.

Magner D 2004 *Magner's Classic Encyclopedia of the Horse* Edison, New Jersey: Castle Books

McGreevy P 2004 *Equine Behavior: A Guide for Veterinarians and Equine Scientists* Philadelphia: Elsevier Limited. ISBN 0 7020 2634 4

McGreevy P, McLean A 2010 *Equitation Science,* Wiley

Blackwell, UK, ISBN 2009048321

McGreevy PD et al 2007 *Roles of Learning theory and ethology in equitation* Journal of Veterinary Behavior 2:108-118

McGreevy PD 2006 *The advent of equitation science* The Veterinary Journal 174:492-500

Waran N, McGreevy P & Casey RA 2002 *Training Methods and Horse Welfare* in Waran N, ed *The Welfare of Horses*, Dordrecht, The Netherlands: Kluwer Academic Publishers, p151-180

Figure 12 The author at 14 atop Belle, a two year Quarter Horse raised on his family ranch in Montana. They are travelling over the Continental Divide at Badger Pass in the Bob Marshall Wilderness. Each year Sid and his father and siblings would bring a string of young horses into the mountains to train and to see the world. It was in these settings that DrSid came to see the world as horses see the world.

In conclusion:

Horses require abundant lifelong friends, forage, and locomotion for health and prosperity. When horses are stabled these requirements have to be appropriately provided.

Natural conditions need to be re-created in the stable on a near-constant basis in some fashion or the other. All horses require miles of daily walking. Abundant daily walking supports all aspects of equine physical and behavioural health.

Figure 13 Walking

Figure 14 Sleipnir Publishing

Contact: NaturalHorseman@Mac.com
Twitter: @EquusCaballus

Horse Behaviour series
Book 1: The Nature of Horses
Book 2: The Language of Horses
Book 3: The Language of Horsemanship

Sid Gustafson
www.sidgustafson.com
www.twitter.com/sidgustafson
www.Facebook.com/RacehorseAdvocacy
Speaking and presentation engagements: DrSid@icloud.com
Equine Behaviour Services and consultations: sidgustafson@mac.com